Gabe

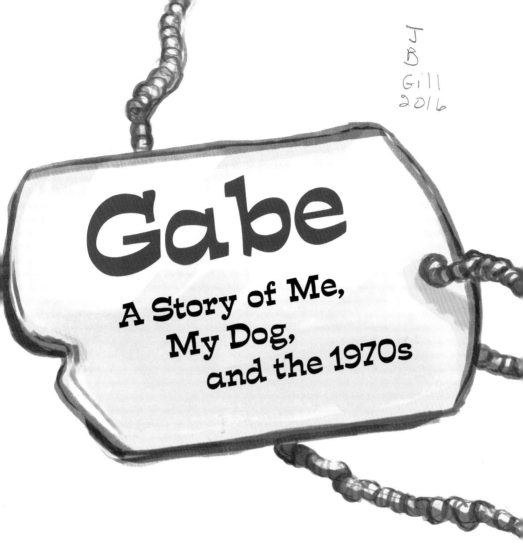

JB Gill 2016

Gabe

A Story of Me, My Dog, and the 1970s

Shelley Gill

Illustrated by **Marc Scheff**

稲 Charlesbridge

1
The Rainbow Gathering

In July 1972 the Rainbow Tribe gathered for the
first time since the huge 1969 rock festival known
as Woodstock. On a mountaintop near Granby,
Colorado, men with long hair, women in flowing
skirts, and naked, happy children camped out,
danced, and celebrated nature, peace, and diversity.
I was there, too, doing first aid.

I left home when I was seventeen.

Florida had nothing I wanted. The once-beautiful beach was polluted, and all anyone cared about was money. Girls were expected to be Barbie, or else. I didn't know where I was going, but I was looking for a more authentic life. The Vietnam War was ending—finally. Now it was peace, love, and rock and roll. The Age of Aquarius.

In 1972 I was volunteering in the medical tent at the first Rainbow Gathering, at Table Mountain near Granby, Colorado. Twenty thousand people were having a blast—except the ones who fell off the steep trail leading up to the plateau.

One crazy biker dude thought he was Evel Knievel and tried to jump his bike off a cliff. The jump went fine, but the landing was rough.

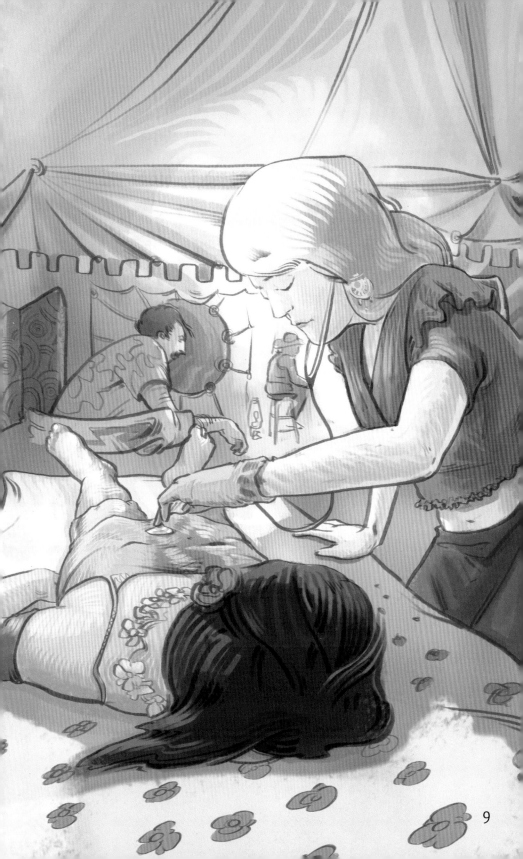

9

Sometimes people's dogs got hurt, too. One pup, a blue merle husky mix with yellow eyes, had a four-inch gash on his left hind leg. His owner left him at the medical tent, then wandered away. I sewed him up and made him a bed next to the crazy biker dude.

When the gathering ended, the people were gone, but the pup was still there. I named him Gabe.

When I left Granby for New Orleans, Gabe came with me. We hitchhiked most of the way. Even as a pup, Gabe was a great judge of character. Before I got in a car, he would leap onto the passenger seat and stare at the driver. If Gabe growled, we didn't take that ride.

2

The Big Easy

Like kids from all over the country, I was drawn to New Orleans, with its warm weather and cool jazz blasting out of bars on Bourbon Street. The cheap food—gumbo, jambalaya, crab po'boys—was spicy. So was life in the

Once we made it to the Big Easy, I rented a cheap
second-floor apartment in the French Quarter. My
neighbor was Madam Dynamite, a huge woman
with purple fingernails and lots of cats.

Gabe stayed home while I worked the night shift at a free medical clinic. We sewed up cuts, lanced boils, and delivered babies. Drugs were everywhere, so we also sat up with bad trips, held hands through withdrawals, and answered the crisis line. On my fourth night at work, my new landlord called—there had been trouble.

I hustled home to find glass in the courtyard and the neighbors gathered below my window. My shutters were splintered, and there was blood on the ground.

Gabe?

Gabe was upstairs in a dark corner, snarling, a torn piece of Levi's at his feet. When he realized it was me, he wagged his tail and pushed his nose into my hand, waiting to be congratulated.

Word hit the mean streets: never break
into Shelley's apartment.

3

On the Move

Back then, nobody on the road had much money, so a lot of kids just hitched rides. A car meant you had to have a place to park it, and that tied you down.

I usually followed the seasons: summer in the Rockies, winter in the south. I worked whatever jobs I could get. I cooked pizza, carried bricks for a mason, and swept up on a construction site. I even worked illegally as a bartender. I never made much money.

From New Orleans we hitched to a concert in Indiana. Then we traveled with a Vietnam Vets Against the War group to protest in New York. I got work on Wall Street to pay for my rent in the Village. Every morning, as I trudged to my boring job answering phones, I struggled to find some sign of nature in all that concrete.

Gabe just struggled. He growled at kids in Central Park and leaned his big gray muzzle against my knee when we got stuck in a crowd. At night he practically slept on my head as lights flashed red in our window and sirens shrieked.

New York wasn't for us.

Kids were moving around all over the country. Home was where your friends were, so Gabe and I became each other's home.

The next spring we were in Colorado, living in a teepee outside Steamboat Springs. Gabe fell in love with the mountains.

And he learned how to fight. When we hiked into town, the town dogs would pack together and attack Gabe. Their leader, Thor, lived at the local general store. He was a burly Rhodesian ridgeback with a Viking attitude.

One day, as I drove up to the store in a friend's car, Gabe sailed through the open window. He hit Thor as the ridgeback was charging the car and forced him back into the store. Up and down the aisles they fought, canned goods raining on their heads, customers screaming, the store owner trying to break it up with a broom.

They were a tornado
of teeth,
tufts of hair,
slobber,
and blood.

As they fought their way toward the door, the owner grabbed the outside pressure hose and turned it on them full blast. They hesitated an instant. I grabbed Gabe's collar and hustled him out.

The next day I went back without Gabe and tried to give the guy all my money: $52. He laughed, and said, "No way." It had been the wildest dogfight he'd seen in forty-five years of western life.

4
Back to the Big Easy

New Orleans was a city of contrasts. Kids new to town usually landed at a crash pad in the French Quarter, where you could pay seventy-five cents for a cot and a bowl of whatever overripe veggies the cooks were able to scrounge from the market at the end of the day. The French Quarter was the dangerous part of town. Drug overdoses and pistol-whippings by the police were common. The health clinic where I worked was there to patch kids up.

The streetcar on St. Charles Avenue took you out of the gritty French Quarter into another world. The Garden District was the New Orleans version of Gone with the Wind—huge mansions with flowers tended by an army of gardeners. It was the last place I wanted to be.

Later that year it was back to New Orleans and a new job at the clinic. Our first night we slept in an old orphanage on the seamy edge of the Garden District.

Gabe was restless. As I headed out on an errand, I warned my roommates not to let him out, but they just had to open the door and take a peek at my mountain dog.

He was through their legs and gone in a flash.

That night I walked the streets calling . . .
crying . . . calling . . . and crying.

I put up posters, alerted the local radio
stations, and combed the alleys and
cobblestone streets night after night. Soon I
had to leave the orphanage to move back to
the French Quarter—but it was miles away.
I lived in a different apartment now, and Gabe
had been to the clinic only once, a year ago.
How would he ever find me?

I kept looking. Then I started to hear strange stories. Radio stations reported that a wolf was loose in the Big Easy—gaunt and dangerous, with big yellow eyes.

"I saw him dumpster diving on St. Charles," one woman called in to say.

"I saw the wolf steal stale bread," a French Market vendor told me.

Folks were getting hysterical. It seemed Gabe had worked his way from the Garden District to the French Quarter. The police said they would shoot him if they could. Bayou boys with shotguns mounted in their rusty pickups were wolf hunting on Canal Street. I had to find Gabe before they did.

I got friends to help me in the worst parts of town. We stumbled over drunks, faced down muggers. My throat ached from calling Gabe's name. Tears stained my face. I was a mess. My ornery blue dog was gone, and I knew in my gut I would never find him.

Two weeks later I was sitting on the grass outside the clinic. A big gray head peered around the corner of the building. I blinked and did a double take.

Gabe!

He cautiously crawled the first few feet, not really believing his eyes. Then he ran and jumped in my lap. He stank like the streets. He *was* gaunt and dangerous looking. But he had found his way back, across a city, to me.

47

5
Alaska

*When I left home, I didn't know where I would end up.
I just trusted that when I got there, I would know it.*

When I was nineteen, Gabe and I finally left the crowds behind and moved to Alaska. I worked as a stonemason. To move the rocks out of the woods, we used dogs.

Where did I get the dogs? Gabe gave them to me.

He fell in love with a malamute named Becca. She had a litter of pups one night and left the next morning. The last I saw of her, she was following a butterfly through the woods.

I bottle-fed the pups. Henry was a blue merle like his dad. Sport was white. Little Becca was gray like her mom. And Ajax had traditional husky markings and sky-blue eyes. They all turned out to be giants.

When we weren't hauling rock, the whole pack of us explored the wilderness, trekking through the Chugach Mountains and hiking knife-ridged trails high in Denali country. Gabe raced through belly-deep snow as I learned to ski the frozen rivers and camp out under the northern lights.

Filled with wonder, the two of us
would curl together in front of the fire,
my hand clutching the hair of his ruff,
my head resting on his chest. His strong
heart would thump loudly in my ear.

Alaska was big and wild and full of possibilities. And it was the end of the road. It seemed too vital to ever be tamed, and it would take a lifetime to explore.

We never left. Gabe and I had finally found home and family, together.

Afterword

The first Iditarod race from Anchorage to Nome was run in 1973.
It's still about the best adventure you can have in Alaska.
It celebrates history, the Native people, and the land.
Joe Redington Sr., known as the Father of the Iditarod,
taught me how to run dogs. Another adventurer, Norman
Vaughan, had been on the 1928 Byrd expedition to the South
Pole. He was a great pal and mentor. Those two men taught
me not only how to live in the wilderness, but also how to live!
They didn't ask, "Why?" They asked, "Why not?"

By 1977, when I was twenty-two, I was living in a wall tent at a camp near Point Mackenzie. I shared the tent with Gabe, a Siamese cat named Mammete, and my friend Susan Butcher. Outside were 130 racing dogs. Susan and I had both signed up to race in the 1,150-mile Iditarod Trail Sled Dog Race as rookies.

The first time I hooked Gabe into lead, it took just minutes for him to learn the commands. But he was too big and slow for racing. When he would take off, the swing dogs would quickly outrun him. His dignity couldn't handle it, so he'd turn and lay into them. You can't have a fighter in harness, so Gabe was off the team. He spent his days in the tent, hanging with Mammete.

Sled dog or not, Gabe was my best friend. He'd been a part of my life since I was seventeen. He had survived my marriage and divorce, seven cities, and a life in bush Alaska.

When I moved to Homer, Alaska, in 1982, Gabe was so old he had to be carried outside morning and night to pee. He made it through an icy winter, scrambling to stay up as he did his business. But by spring it was obvious that his time had come.

Gabe lived to be seventeen years old.

He died quickly and painlessly, his rear legs crippled, his eyes gone foggy with age. He spent his last moments with his body spooned against mine, his gray ruff tickling my chin, his heart thumping slowly, the way we had so often slept along the trail.

Signs of the Times

The Vietnam War
In 1955 the United States joined South Vietnam in its struggle against the communist forces of North Vietnam. As the war dragged on, public opinion turned against the war. Young people were especially suspicious of our leaders' motives. During World War II the enemy was obvious. Japanese pilots bombed the US naval base in Pearl Harbor, Hawaii. Adolf Hitler and his German Nazis dreamed of worldwide domination. Americans pulled together to fight against these enemies. But Southeast Asia was a different story. What were we fighting for?

Protesting the war
Emotions about the Vietnam War ran high. Protesters spit on returning veterans and called them turncoats and baby-killers, even though most were drafted into service. On May 4, 1970, four unarmed students protesting US involvement in the war were shot down by the National Guard at Kent State University. The Vietnam Veterans Against the War had seen the conflict firsthand and could not defend their country's actions in that far-off jungle. They called for peace and an end to the war. In 1973 the United States began withdrawing its forces from Vietnam. On April 30, 1975, Saigon, the capital of South Vietnam, fell, bringing an end to a long and bloody war.

The Civil Rights Movement
In the late 1960s black and brown Americans were fighting for simple rights—equal education, a fair judicial system, and the right to eat in restaurants, sit on any bus seats they chose, and use bathrooms that were labeled "Whites Only." Every day people saw the way some Americans were ill-treated in this land of the free and home of the brave, and many of us joined the fight.

The Civil Rights Act had banned discrimination based on skin color in 1964, but racist violence was still rampant. Black children were murdered, churches were bombed, and black and white election workers were hunted down by the Ku Klux Klan. Some civil rights leaders, like Martin Luther King Jr., argued for a nonviolent solution to the conflict. Other leaders, like Huey Newton of the Black Panther Party, preached "black power" and urged their followers to fight for liberation.

The Women's Movement
Women were fighting for fair treatment, too. The Equal Rights Amendment (ERA), which would guarantee women the same rights as men, was passed by Congress in 1972 and sent to the states for ratification. If thirty-eight of the states approved, the ERA would become the newest amendment to the Constitution. Unfortunately, due to pressure from anti-ERA organizers, not enough states ratified the amendment and it was defeated. But the fight wasn't over! In 1982, the ERA was reintroduced in Congress, and it has been debated in every session since.

The Age of Aquarius
The Vietnam War and the fight for civil rights had changed kids growing up in America. Many really believed it was the dawning of a new age devoted to peace, equality, protecting the environment, and living a simpler, more sustainable life. We welcomed the Age of Aquarius with a deep sense of optimism and empowerment. We could change the world!

For Benj and Mike, aka The Boys, who have made my journey so much sweeter, and for my darling daughter, Kye, who inspires me every day in every way. And to Mary Cobb, Sean Barrett, Meg Pettibone, Mitch Vandiver, Hobbit, Chuck Hathaway, and Peggy Vagabond—thanks for sharing this chapter in the life of Shelley.—S. G.

To my two huskies, Phoenix and Bailey, who were very patient models. And to Chloe, who makes this adventure worth living, every day.—M. S.

Text copyright © 2016 by Shelley Gill
Illustrations copyright © 2016 by Marc Scheff
All rights reserved, including the right of reproduction in whole or in part in any form. Charlesbridge and colophon are registered trademarks of Charlesbridge Publishing, Inc.

Published by Charlesbridge, 85 Main Street, Watertown, MA 02472
(617) 926-0329 • www.charlesbridge.com

Library of Congress Cataloging-in-Publication Data
Gill, Shelley.
    Gabe: a story of me, my dog, and the 1970s / Shelley Gill; illustrated by Marc Scheff.
        pages cm
    ISBN 978-1-57091-354-9 (reinforced for library use)
    ISBN 978-1-60734-645-6 (ebook)
    ISBN 978-1-60734-762-0 (ebook pdf)
    1. Dogs—United States—Biography—Juvenile literature. 2. Gill, Shelley—Childhood and youth—Juvenile literature. 3. Human-animal relationships—Juvenile literature. 4. Granby (Colo.)—Biography—Juvenile literature. 5. New Orleans (La.)—Biography—Juvenile literature. 6. Alaska—Biography—Juvenile literature. I. Scheff, Marc, illustrator. II. Title.
    SF426.5.G554 2016
    636.70092—dc23   2014049185

Printed in China
(hc) 10 9 8 7 6 5 4 3 2 1

Illustrations done in pencil on paper, scanned, and finished in Photoshop
Display type set in Estro and text type set in Palatino Sans
Color separations by Colourscan Print Co Pte Ltd, Singapore
Printed by C & C Offset Printing Co. Ltd. in Shenzhen, Guangdong, China
Production supervision by Brian G. Walker
Designed by Susan Mallory Sherman